Red Pandas
For Kids

Amazing Animal Books
For Young Readers

By
Rachel Smith

Mendon Cottage Books
JD-Biz Corp Publishing

All Rights Reserved.

No part of this publication may be reproduced in any form or by any means, including scanning, photocopying, or otherwise without prior written permission from JD-Biz Corp

Copyright © 2015. All Images Licensed by Fotolia and 123RF.

Read More Amazing Animal Books

Purchase at Amazon.com

Table of Contents

Introduction

The red panda is probably one of the cutest creatures around, easily tying with the giant panda. But why are they both called pandas if they look so incredibly different? And what makes the red panda different from, say, a raccoon?

Red pandas are unique animals all their own. They live in Asia, towards the East, and they have been a more recent favorite animal of many children and adults. Unlike its name-sibling the giant panda, the red panda receives less attention than many endangered animals. However, it is also one of the more common zoo animals, since red pandas do so well in zoos.

What makes the red panda an animal worth knowing? There are a lot of answers to that question, and we will cover them in this book.

What is a red panda?

A red panda is a unique animal. It's also known as the lesser panda, the red bear cat and the red cat bear. As you can see, just from the names, there has been a lot of confusion as to what exactly the red panda is.

A red panda relaxing on a tree branch.

To start off, the red panda is a mammal. A mammal is an animal that is warm-blooded and nurses its young; many mammals also have fur or hair, though this is not always true, as the blue whale is a mammal too. However, the blue whale is certainly not hairy or furry.

Beyond that, a red panda is called Ailurus Fulgens. That is its scientific name, a name that scientists use to refer to it, usually based in dead languages such as Latin or Ancient Greek. Now, it may seem silly to use languages like that to name every animal, but it's actually a pretty cool way to do it. It means that it's the same for every scientist, no matter what language they speak. This works whether it's Japanese, English, or Khalkha Mongolian.

Ailurus Fulgens is the only animal in its genus, or even in its family. The red panda is truly unique, not closely related to seemingly any other animal.

Another thing about the red panda is that it is not a carnivore. It is an omnivore, meaning that it eats a variety of things. One of these things, the main thing, is bamboo. Other things are a large group.

The red panda is not a large animal. It's a bit larger than a domestic cat, or a house cat. If you've seen a cat, then just imagine this animal being a little bigger.

One very recognizable thing about the red panda is its coloring. Its ringed tail definitely catches your attention, and its face is marked red on white in many cases. In fact, in some areas, it is called the fire fox for its brilliantly red coloring.

Its ears are upright and kind of large; its eyes are very darkly colored. The red panda has sharp claws that are semi-retractable, meaning they can kind of pull them in a bit. They are very strong claws meant for climbing.

A red panda can also rotate its ankle. This is something few animals can do, and it helps them climb trees. You'll very often find red pandas in trees, and unlike domestic cats, they can climb down them face-forward. This is a reason cats often get stuck in trees: they can climb up, but their claws face the wrong way to climb down, and they haven't master climbing down backwards. The red panda simply rotates its ankle to climb down.

One thing that the giant panda and the red panda have in common is a false thumb. The false thumb comes from its wrist, instead of part of its hand like in a human. That's why it's called a false thumb.

The white area and the ringed tail of the red panda have long made people assume it's related to the raccoon. Other things, such as bamboo-eating and the false thumb, have made people think it's related to the giant panda.

Neither is really an accurate assessment.

How do red pandas act?

Red pandas are solitary creatures. This means they don't really live in groups, and like to have their space. They are territorial, meaning that they have an area they defend and keep for themselves.

A red panda.

Red pandas don't make very many sounds. Twittering, whistling sounds tend to be it, and even those aren't made very often. This is because they're not often in contact with each other, so there's little reason to try to communicate. It is a very quiet species, which is probably why the red panda is not included in books about animal sounds.

They like to sleep in trees, because they are creatures that are very good at climbing and they feel safe there. It sleeps one of two ways, generally speaking: sprawled and limbs hanging, so that it can cool down, or curled up with its tail on its face, to warm up.

One reason that red pandas do things like sleep in trees is because they have a number of predators. Unlike creatures like, for example, the jaguar, red pandas are not apex predators. An apex predator is a carnivore or hunting animal of some kind that has no natural enemies, other than possibly humans. A red panda is not one of these at all.

One of the better known predators of the red panda is the snow leopard. Both are beautiful species and somewhat endangered. The snow leopard is an apex predator. Another predator of the red panda is the marten. A marten is actually somewhat related to the red panda, but it's the more dangerous animal and will eat the red panda if it gets the chance.

The last main predators of the red panda are humans. That's an entirely different thing than the hunting done by snow leopards and martens, however.

Red pandas are not very good at handling different temperatures. They need to be at a sort of lukewarm temperature, somewhere between seventeen and twenty-five degrees Celsius, or in the sixties or seventies Fahrenheit. It does its best at these temperatures. Now, a red panda can survive in other temperatures, but it really doesn't do well about about twenty-five degrees Celsius, or seventy-seven degrees Fahrenheit.

When they wake up in the morning, red pandas tend to groom themselves, licking their paws and fur. This is kind of like house cats, which is another reason there is so much confusion about where the red panda belongs in the animal family.

Then, after doing this grooming routine, a red panda will make its territory again, rubbing its body against things like trees and rocks. They also use urine (pee) and a special scent that comes from their anal glands (glands in the rear end) to mark their territory.

Red pandas, despite their sharp claws, are not really fighters. They tend to run when they feel scared, heading up a tree or something else they can climb. When they can't run, instead, they stand on their back paws and try to look big. This is when they will use their claws to fight, though they much prefer not to.

Like their name-sibling the giant panda, a red panda relies heavily on bamboo for food. Also like the giant panda, the red panda can't digest cellulose. Cellulose is what makes up much of a plant, and since bamboo is a plant, it makes up much of the food that red pandas eat. This means that a red panda doesn't even use a huge portion of what it eats, and this is why both giant pandas and red pandas must eat an enormous amount of bamboo a day.

However, red pandas don't just eat bamboo. They may eat berries, flowers, eggs, small mammals, or other things. In zoos, they've been known to eat the leaves of certain kinds of trees. This is why the red panda is classified as an omnivore and not an herbivore, which is a creature that strictly eats plants.

One interesting little fact is that red pandas can taste artificial sweeteners. Artificial sweeteners are sort of like sugar, except man-made. Most animals can't taste them besides primates, like chimpanzees.

Red pandas reproduce during one time period a year, from part of January to part of March. The red panda is not fond of other adult red pandas, and prefers to have its own space; however, during this time period, a red panda may mate with several other red pandas.

Females are tasked with raising the young; sometimes, when they live in groups or pairs (such as in a zoo), a male may show interest in the cubs. However, most often, a red panda father never even meets its cubs.

A female red panda carries its babies for a bit less time than humans by a couple months. When she knows she's going to give birth soon, she starts to make a nest. She gathers soft things and waits patiently.

When the cubs are born, they are blind and deaf. There are typically one or two, barring some unusual exception. The mother stays with them for a huge amount of her time the first week. However, as time goes on, she leaves them alone for longer and longer. She always returns to feed and groom her cubs, however.

Even as soon as shortly after birth, a mother red panda can tell her cubs apart by their scents. She often moves them to different nests,. She typically has about three or four nests to keep her cubs in.

These cubs slowly get their adult coloring, the dark red-brown color of its parents. They also mature fairly fast compared to a human, being ready to have babies at eighteen months of age, though they are only full adults at two or three years old.

The cubs are weaned (shifted from their mother's milk to solid foods) at six or eight months. By the time the next batch of cubs is born the next summer, it is time for the older cubs to go. However, they are ready to take on the world by this point.

A red panda will typically live about eight or ten years, though some have been known to live as long as fifteen years. This is more often a captive animal.

Where do red pandas live?

Red pandas live in a specific part of Asia. The Himalayas, a range of mountains, have many forests around them, and it's here that the red panda is endemic, meaning that it stays in this area and is native to this area.

A red panda in the snow.

The Himalayas are in part of China, Nepal, and other places. For example, much of Nepal has the Himalayan Mountains, and there is a lot of industry based around mountain climbing in those areas.

However, because China is such a big country, it's only a very small portion of it that has the Himalayas. Tibet is the main area that has the

Himalayas. It's currently a part of China, though that's a very complicated issue. Tibet has less of a mountain climbing industry than Nepal.

The red panda does not live only in the area of Himalayas, but rather in the foothills and mountains surrounding it too. This means that its territory goes all the way into India, Burma, and Bhutan as well, all Asian countries with their own unique cultures. India is one of the most populous countries in the world, and has been well-known for things such as the number of gods there are in the Hindu religion, which is native to India, and for their distinctive women's dress, the sari.

Bhutan is less well-known, being a smaller country. However, it is rated as the happiest Asian country, and has a very unspoiled environment. This is an excellent place for the red panda to live, due to the protection of the environment.

Burma, also known as Myanmar, has less of that. Burma has long had strife throughout its lands, and in fact had one of the longest civil wars. In some ways, Burma has a lot more environmental problems than Bhutan. However, there is still a lot of undisturbed wilderness in Burma.

What kinds of red pandas are there?

There are two subspecies of red panda. One is the western red panda, and the other is Styan's red panda.

A red panda making a face.

The important thing to know about subspecies is that they are simply kinds of a species that are a little different from each other. For example, there are a number of subspecies of tiger, from the Siberian to the Bengal.

Red panda subspecies are very similar, and most people would not be able to tell them apart.

Styan's red panda is said to be a bit bigger and darker, with differences in its skull and teeth. It's said to live in the China and Burma part of the range, on one side of a river that separates the two.

The western red panda, on the other hand, lives more in India, Bhutan, and Nepal.

Altogether, though, there is a lot of debate about whether these subspecies actually exist, or if there's just a single species involved.

The history of red pandas and humans

Humans and red pandas have generally gotten along. The red panda is not the victim of an extreme amount of habitat damage, though there is damage, and it's not at the center of extreme hunting.

A sleeping red panda.

However, there are only about ten thousand in the wild. Surprisingly, this is not due to a loss of territory; in fact, even though there has been some territory lost, red pandas only use about half of the available territory.

The red panda is protected by all the countries it lives in, and efforts have been made to make the number of red pandas go higher.

One main issue with the deforestation that has taken place is the inbreeding of the red pandas. Because they are now in smaller groups with less access to other pandas, they tend to breed within their own group. Inbreeding means that there's less genetic diversity.

For example, with humans, there would be a problem if there were only fifty people ever in one space. They would be similar genetically and more likely to have genetic illnesses. The biggest problem with in-breeding is that if everyone's similar, when a new disease strikes, it may wipe them all out because they are the same. Within a diverse group, it's more likely that someone will have the genes, or the genetic ability, to not die from the disease.

That's the reason people survived the Black Death way back in the Middle Ages. The Black Death was a disease that enveloped much of the world in a pandemic; a pandemic is when a disease is spread over many areas in large numbers. This was very common in older times because of bad hygiene and sanitation (sanitation being stuff like washing your hands and cleaning tools and such). People would literally throw their urine and feces into the street back then.

Another problem for the red panda is that it is sometimes poached, dead or alive. It's valuable due to its exotic nature; a lot of people who collect animals find animals from this area of the world 'exotic,' when they are just part of life for people who actually live there.

Another reason it's valuable is for the Chinese people. Red panda tails are often used for good luck hats in Chinese wedding ceremonies, and have been for hundreds of years. The skin is also valuable for this reason.

The Nepalese have no known traditions around the red panda. They have not been known to hunt them in the same way as the Chinese.

A Nepalese village actually works to take care of a forest with about fifteen red pandas in it. These pandas are helped to survive, and in turn, help the villagers survive. How, you might ask? Through tourism; people will come great distances to see the red pandas.

A group of five villages in India have also banded together to protect the red pandas in their area.

Red pandas are still very much the target of poachers, though not quite as much as animals like tigers and elephants. They are very valuable, though they are typically sold alive rather than as a skin like with many tigers and other big cats.

The genetic debate

There is a lot of debate as to what genetic group the red panda belongs to. Early on, it has been put into groups including cats, bears, and the family that includes raccoons.

A raccoon.

The first time the red panda was described, or noted, by an animal expert, it was put in the raccoon family, Procyonidae. It also includes other New World (South or North American) animals, such as the coati and the kinkajou.

This is an unusual choice, because all the other animals that belong to that family live in North America. It seems the man who first classified them thought that because of its ringed tail and other similarities to raccoons that made it related. Another thing is that he thought it acted very much like a cat, and its scientific named also has a word that means cat in it.

After that, it was put into the Ursidae family, which is the family of bears.

It was also put into the Ailuropodinae, which was at the time the family of both the giant panda and the red panda. This family was moved into the Ursidae family. Strangely, even though the giant panda eats bamboo mainly, and is mostly an herbivore (plant eater), it is still a bear.

The red panda has been classified as belonging to the same family as the giant panda because they both eat copious amounts of bamboo, and not much else.

It now belongs to its own family, Ailuridae.

One interesting thing about this journey for the red panda is the origin of its name. We're not entirely sure where the word 'panda' actually comes from. It's believed that this was chosen due to the French name of the Roman Goddess, Panda. She was considered the goddess to call on for a difficult journey.

However, later texts claim that panda came from a local word.

Another interesting thing is that the red panda was almost called the 'wha.' According to the man suggesting this name, this was what the local people called it, and this was the sound it made.

However, his paper on it was not published in time, and another man had already proposed a name that was generally accepted by the time he got it published.

Red pandas as pets

Red pandas, since they are around the size of a house pet, have long been popular as pets among the peoples who live in and near their habitat.

A red panda looking out.

At first, it must sound like a really fun idea to have a red panda as a pet. However, there are a lot of issues with it.

The first is that the red panda is a wild animal. It's generally a bad idea to take in a wild animal as a pet, because wild animals belong in the wild. It's where they will be happiest. Most people can't offer the kind of habitat it needs, nor meet its other needs.

Another thing is that bamboo in the quantities it needs is quite expensive.

More important is that it is a nocturnal, solitary creature. Unlike a dog, it won't want to be cuddled, and will probably want to be left alone most of the time. It also would not around during the day, instead sleeping for much of it. Unless the owner happens to stay up all night, he or she would barely see them.

Lastly, it needs much more space than most people can offer. It's different among people who live near them; they don't try to trap them into staying. They're allowed to have full range, and they don't try to alter the red panda into some kind of dog or cat.

The red panda, first and foremost, belongs in the wild.

Conclusion

Red pandas are cute, some of the most adorable animals in the world. They don't have a lot to do with much of the culture in the world, but they are very important where they do live.

We can only hope that they make it, with the danger their species is in.

Author Bio

Rachel Smith is a young author who enjoys animals. Once, she had a rabbit which was very nervous, and chewed through her leash and tried to escape. She's also had several pet mice, which were the funniest little animals to watch. She lives in Ohio with her family and writes in her spare time.

Publisher

JD-Biz Corp

P O Box 374

Mendon, Utah 84325

http://www.jd-biz.com/

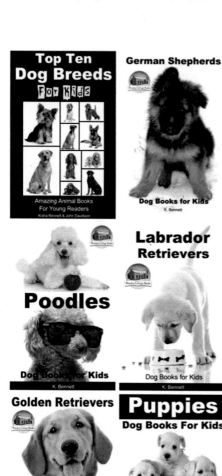

32539241R00020

Made in the USA
San Bernardino, CA
08 April 2016